Sharing the Word

I0152229

Torn Asunder
A Biblical Look
at Divorce and Remarriage

Clay A. Kahler

Wipf & Stock
PUBLISHERS
Eugene, Oregon

Torn Asunder – A Biblical Look at Divorce and Remarriage
(Sharing the Word Series)
Copyright © 2005 by Dr. Clay A. Kahler

Wipf and Stock Publishers
199 W 8th Ave, Suite 3
Eugene, OR 97401

Torn Asunder
A Biblical Look at Divorce and Remarriage
By Kahler, Clay A.
Copyright©2006 by Kahler, Clay A.
ISBN: 1-59752-807-2
Publication date 3/1/2006

ACKNOWLEDGEMENTS

There are many people to whom I owe a great debt. First to my many learned seminary professors who taught me well both inside the classroom and outside of it as well. These great men not only taught me Bible and Theology, but more importantly they taught me to think.

Dr. George Goolde

Dr. Gary Coombs

Dr. George Hare

Dr. David Myers

Dr. Garland Shin

Dr. Tony Crisp

Prof. Thomas Rohm

Then I owe the members and leaders of the First Baptist Church of Orrick MO. for their patience and their love. It is a privilege to serve as your pastor and I hope to continue until the Lord comes back.

Finally I want to thank Becky Thomas for her tireless proof reading of this manuscript. Trying to catch all of my typos and mistakes cannot be an easy task. As the great theologian Forrest Gump said, "I know that I am not a smart man."

Table of Contents

I just read that last year 4,153,237 people got married in the U.S. I don't want to start any trouble, but shouldn't that be an even number?

Introduction

The Divorce Myth

Controversy is rampant in the Christian community in many areas. We argue over such topics as the time of the rapture, the millennium, or no millennium, Dispensationalism versus Covenantalism. However, no issue stirs up good people to hard feelings like the subject of divorce and remarriage.

Many good people in ministry find themselves on opposite sides of this issue. J. Carl Laney, author of *The Divorce Myth* and professor at Western Conservative Baptist Seminary states that there is no place for divorce or remarriage. On divorce and remarriage he writes,

We can conclude the following: (1) the original creative intention and desired will of God is that marriage be permanent until death; (2) neither God Himself nor God through Moses commanded divorce; (3) the explanation the New Testament gives for allowing divorce in the Old Testament is the hardness of the people's heart-hearts unsubmitted to the restraints of a high and holy God.... When a divorce does occur, the only two scriptural options for the divorced person are reconciliation or the single life.[1]

William A. Heth, assistant professor of New Testament and Greek at Taylor University and coauthor of *Jesus and Divorce* believes that Divorce is allowed but no remarriage. He writes,

Even though marital separation or legal divorce may be advisable under some circumstances, Jesus taught that His disciples should not remarry after divorce. This would be contrary to the nature of marriage as God designed it in his creation and a violation of

---

[1] House, H. Wayne Ed., Divorce and Remarriage Four Christian Views. Downers Grove: Intervarsity Press, 1990. p16

the seventh commandment: "You shall not commit adultery."[2]

Dr. Lawrence O. Richards of Wheaton College, states that divorce and remarriage are allowable under a variety of circumstances.

The fact remains that there is little agreement on this explosive subject. However, as long as ministers and counselors have to deal with a fallen people, divorce and remarriage will be a bitter part of Christendom. So let us look into Scripture and determine God's answer to this question.

If there were an unforgivable sin according to many in the church today, it would be divorce. But what does scripture say? The Body of Christ today, needs reliable biblically based information.

In this work, I will attempt to offer help in the midst of all the confusion. I come to this difficult subject with careful attention to the biblical issues. After many years in pastoral ministry I have seen that in the minds of many Christians, divorce is the only unforgivable sin. I hope that after careful and thorough examination of the Biblical texts on the subject that this issue may be clearer to myself as well as to the reader.

---

[2] Heth, W.A. and G.J. Wenham, *Jesus and Divorce*. London: Hodder and Stroughton, 1984. p73

The purpose of this work is to determine what the biblical record has to say concerning divorce and remarriage. In the process many questions will be explored, such as: Does the Bible allow for divorce in any circumstance? If so, is there ever provision for remarriage. Finally, can one who has been divorced and remarried serve as a church leader, specifically as Pastor?

Chapter 1

Mixed Signals

Some students of Scripture say that the Bible gives no grounds for divorce or remarriage. Others suggest that the Bible allows for divorce under some circumstances but does not allow for remarriage. Some say that if a divorce is justified, so is the possibility of remarriage. Still others say that God's primary concern is our happiness.

In the following pages, I will attempt to offer help in the midst of all the confusion. I come to this difficult subject not only as a married man and as a minister of the Gospel ministry, but also with careful attention to the biblical issues. After having conducted dozens of marriages and providing many hours of marital counseling, I have come to conclusions that combine reverence for the Scriptures with compassion for those whose marital hopes have turned into regret and loss.

Mixed Signals

Divorce statistics can be confusing. On one hand, we are told that nearly one of every two marriages will end in divorce[3]. What we observe seems to bear this out. Far more children than in the past are growing up in single-parent families[4]. On the other hand, we are told that the divorced segment of our population only equals about 12 percent of the married segment. According to *Grolier's Encyclopedia*, "In the United States in 1987, there were 123 divorced persons for every 1,000 married persons.[5]"

---

[3] The last-reported U.S. divorce rate of which we are aware is 0.41% per capita per year, the provisional estimate for the year 2000 from the National Center for Health Statistics. Since every divorce involves two people, the percentage becomes somewhat more meaningful if you double it. A rate per married people, instead of per straight population, would be even more helpful. *PER CAPITA ANNUAL.*: Monthly Vital Statistics Report, Vol. 49, No. 6

[4] According to the "Marital Status and Living Arrangements: March 1998 Update" by Terry A. Lugaila: at the US Census Bureau: As of March 1998 Current Population Survey, 19.8 million children under the age of 18 lived with one parent-this translates to 27.7 percent of all children under the age of 18. 84.1 percent of children who lived with a single parent, lived with their mother. Approximately 40.3 percent of these kids lived with a mother who had never been married. About 15.9 percent of children from a single parent household lived with their father. Children who lived with their father only were more likely to be living with a divorced dad (44.4 percent) than a never-married dad (33.3 percent). 55.7 percent of children living with a single parent were living in a household where there is one adult. About 4 million children lived in the household of their grandparents, representing 5.6 percent of all children under 18. 1.4 million of these kids had no parent present in the home.

[5] 2002 Grolier Multimedia Encyclopedia Deluxe

Public opinion expert Louis Harris offers an explanation. He says, "The fact is that in 1981 the number of divorces did hit a record total of 1,213,000. Marriages also reached a record of 2,422,000. Some quick-read experts then put the two sets of facts together and concluded that since there were half as many divorces as marriages, it could be concluded that half of the marriages were doomed to failure. But the facts show that only 10% of all ever-married men and a slightly higher 13% of all ever-married women are divorced."[6]

Mixed signals also come from the painful experiences of life. During my time as a pastor, I have been involved with numerous divorce situations. Sometimes, as in cases of extreme mental or physical abuse, I longed to see a woman become freed from the terror of an abusive husband. Yet, I was uncomfortable advising action that had no clear biblical grounds for divorce and remarriage. In some cases, I wanted to help the abusive husband overcome his problem. Changed lives seemed more preferable than divorce that would divide children, friends, and family assets.

The confusion over divorce, however, is not just rooted in statistics, or even experience. Mixed signals are also found in the Bible. On one hand, the Old Testament prophet Malachi declared, "The LORD God of Israel says that He hates divorce" (Mal. 2:16).

---

[6] Harris , Louis, *Inside America*, New York Vintage Books, 1987, p.86

Yet, God Himself admits to divorcing Israel:

> Then I saw that for all the causes for which backsliding Israel had committed adultery, I had put her away and given her a certificate of divorce; yet her treacherous sister Judah did not fear, but went and played the harlot also. -Jer. 3:8

On one occasion, the prophet Ezra insisted that the men of Israel divorce the pagan wives they had married:

> Then Ezra the priest stood up and said to them, "You have transgressed and have taken pagan wives, adding to the guilt of Israel. Now therefore, make confession to the LORD God of your fathers, and do His will; separate yourselves from the peoples of the land, and from the pagan wives." -Ezra 10:10-11

Later, Jesus said that sexual immorality is the only grounds for divorce:

> And I say to you, whoever divorces his wife, except for sexual immorality, and marries another, commits adultery; and

whoever marries her who is divorced commits adultery." -Mt. 19:9

Yet, the apostle Paul taught that divorce is also permissible if a Christian is married to a non-Christian who no longer wants to be married:

> But if the unbeliever departs, let him depart; a brother or a sister is not under bondage in such *cases*. But God has called us to peace. -1 Cor. 7:15

If one does not account for the dispensational implications[7], this sort of confusion is imminent.

Does the Bible contradict itself about divorce? No. Even though many godly Bible students disagree on what the Bible teaches about divorce and remarriage, I believe the Scriptures offer guidelines for those facing divorce and remarriage. Even in cases of physical abuse, which has become such a troubling issue in our day, I am convinced that the Bible gives us the answers.

---

[7] Dispensationalism is the result of a system of interpretation that seeks to establish a unity in the Scriptures through its central focus on the grace of God. Although dispensationalists recognize differing stewardships or dispensations whereby the Lord put man under a trust, they teach that response to God's revelation in each dispensation is by faith (salvation is *always* by grace through faith). Dispensationalists arrive at their system of interpretation through two primary principles: (1) maintaining a consistently literal, grammatical, and historical method of interpretation, and (2) maintaining a distinction between Israel and the church.
(For further study also see the author's *Simple Theology: Theology for the Rest of us*; and *Dispensationalism* by Charles Ryrie.)

Chapter 2

The Divine Guidance

While God desires that a husband and wife stay together until death, He permits divorce in some circumstances. Three Bible passages give us His guidelines on this matter. They are: *Deuteronomy 24:1-4, Matthew 19:1-10,* and *1 Corinthians 7:10-16.* We will study each passage, taking into consideration the historical situation, the provision made, and the restriction imposed.

> When a man takes a wife and marries her,
> and it happens that she finds no favor in his
> eyes because he has found some uncleanness

in her, and he writes her a certificate of divorce, puts it in her hand, and sends her out of his house, when she has departed from his house, and goes and becomes another man's wife, if the latter husband detests her and writes her a certificate of divorce, puts it in her hand, and sends her out of his house, or if the latter husband dies who took her as his wife, then her former husband who divorced her must not take her back to be his wife after she has been defiled; for that is an abomination before the LORD, and you shall not bring sin on the land which the LORD your God is giving you as an inheritance. -Deuteronomy 24:1-4

In this passage, Moses declared that after a man had divorced his wife because he had found "some uncleanness" in her and both had entered new marriages, they could not dissolve the new marriages and marry each other a second time. Men apparently were already divorcing their wives for "some uncleanness." We don't know when Moses began allowing such divorce, but that he had done so previous to the writing of Deuteronomy 24 is clear. Jesus, some 1,500 years later, told a group of Jewish leaders, "Moses, because of the hardness of your hearts, *permitted* you to divorce your wives" (Mt. 19:8, *italics mine*).

It is certainly correct to say that in the Scriptures God acknowledges the existence of divorce and carefully regulates it. Our stance, then, must be the same. "We must neither wink at divorce, nor simply denounce it (both extremes are unbiblical)."[8]

The Historical Situation.

At the time of Moses and throughout the Old Testament era, a man became the master of the woman he married. This was true in all the cultures of the time, even among the Israelites. A wife was a husband's possession in a manner similar to his property, his animals, and his slaves:

> You shall not covet your neighbor's house;
> you shall not covet your neighbor's wife,
> nor his male servant, nor his female servant,
> nor his ox, nor his donkey, nor anything that
> is your neighbor's. -Ex. 20:17

Jewish law did not permit a woman to initiate a divorce. She could remarry only if given a certificate of

---

[8] Adams, Jay E., Marriage Divorce and Remarriage in the Bible. Grand Rapids: Zondervan Publishing House, 1980, p.28

divorce. Any promise she made could be overruled by her husband:

> If indeed she takes a husband, while bound by her vows or by a rash utterance from her lips by which she bound herself, and her husband hears it, and makes no response to her on the day that he hears, then her vows shall stand, and her agreements by which she bound herself shall stand. But if her husband overrules her on the day that he hears it, he shall make void her vow which she took and what she uttered with her lips, by which she bound herself, and the LORD will release her. -Num. 30:6-8

The husband could have his bride stoned if on the wedding night he discovered that she was not a virgin:

> If any man takes a wife, and goes in to her, and detests her, and charges her with shameful conduct, and brings a bad name on her, and says, "I took this woman, and when I came to her I found she was not a virgin," then the father and mother of the young woman shall take and bring out the evidence of the young woman's virginity to the elders of the city at the gate. And the

young woman's father shall say to the elders, "I gave my daughter to this man as wife, and he detests her. Now he has charged her with shameful conduct, saying, 'I found your daughter was not a virgin,' and yet these are the evidences of my daughter's virginity." And they shall spread the cloth before the elders of the city. Then the elders of that city shall take that man and punish him; and they shall fine him one hundred shekels of silver and give them to the father of the young woman, because he has brought a bad name on a virgin of Israel. And she shall be his wife; he cannot divorce her all his days. But if the thing is true, and evidences of virginity are not found for the young woman, then they shall bring out the young woman to the door of her father's house, and the men of her city shall stone her to death with stones, because she has done a disgraceful thing in Israel, to play the harlot in her father's house. So you shall put away the evil from among you. -Dt. 22:13-21

The society in Israel was definitely patriarchal like that of neighboring nations.

God, however, did not permit men unlimited power over their wives. They could not sell a wife into slavery, like neighboring nations could. Not even if she were a war prisoner who had been made a secondary wife:

> When you go out to war against your enemies, and the LORD your God delivers them into your hand, and you take them captive, and you see among the captives a beautiful woman, and desire her and would take her for your wife, then you shall bring her home to your house, and she shall shave her head and trim her nails. She shall put off the clothes of her captivity, remain in your house, and mourn her father and her mother a full month; after that you may go in to her and be her husband, and she shall be your wife. And it shall be, if you have no delight in her, then you shall set her free, but you certainly shall not sell her for money; you shall not treat her brutally, because you have humbled her. -Dt. 21:10-14

The children were commanded to honor the mother as well as the father (Ex. 20:12). A man could not humiliate his wife by marrying a sister as a rival (Lev. 18:18). The Lord gave these laws as a merciful provision for women in a male-dominated society. Through these regulations,

God showed the men in Israel that their wives were to be viewed as people, not merely as property.

The Provision Made

Because of the hardness of men's hearts, Moses allowed divorce (Mt. 19:8). In the process, however, God provided guidelines. A man had to obtain a certificate of divorce and give it to the unwanted wife. When he did take such action, the divorce certificate would show that the woman had been legally released from marriage and that she was now free to marry another.

Moses permitted such action if a man found some uncleanness in his wife. The exact meaning of the expression "uncleanness[9]" is not clear. It is a word that was almost always translated "nakedness" by the King James translators. An exception is when the word was used to describe an "unclean camp" in which human excrement had not been properly buried:

> For the LORD your God walks in the midst
> of your camp, to deliver you and give your
> enemies over to you; therefore your camp
> shall be holy, that He may see no unclean

---

[9] *Strong's Hebrew and Greek Dictionaries:* H6172 ervâh From H6168; *nudity,* literally (especially the *pudenda*) or figuratively (*disgrace, blemish*): nakedness, shame, unclean (-ness).

thing among you, and turn away from you.
-Dt. 23:14

In some cases, as in Leviticus 18 and 20, the word was linked to specific instances of family sexual abuse. Given this usage, it is possible that if a man suspected his wife had been sexually molested by a family member prior to marriage, he could give her a certificate of divorce. Such an allowance might seem unmerciful. But keep in mind that this stipulation was granted because of "hardness of heart" circumstances. If a man could not deal with something that caused his wife to be despised in his eyes, the law allowed for her to be freed rather than to be subject to his contempt.

We know that Moses was not allowing divorce just in instances of adultery, because adultery was an offense punishable by death:

> If a man is found lying with a woman married to a husband, then both of them shall die—the man that lay with the woman, and the woman; so you shall put away the evil from Israel. -Dt. 22:22

The "uncleanness," therefore, must have referred originally to conduct on the part of the wife that the husband deemed shameful or offensive, but not limited to physical adultery. We have no knowledge of how this was interpreted during Israel's early history.

At the time of Christ, Jewish rabbis disagreed about what Moses meant by the expression "some uncleanness." The followers of Rabbi Shammai limited this term to some kind of sexual impropriety (not necessarily adultery). The followers of Rabbi Hillel (the vast majority) gave it almost unlimited latitude, even making minor offenses like burning food a legitimate basis for divorce[10].

The Restriction Imposed

The focus of Deuteronomy 24:1-4 is the following restriction: Once the divorced pair had married new mates,

---

[10] Hillel and Shammai- These two great scholars born a generation or two before the beginning of the Common Era are usually discussed together and contrasted with each other, because they were contemporaries and the leaders of two opposing schools of thought (known as "houses"). The Talmud records over 300 differences of opinion between Beit Hillel (the House of Hillel) and Beit Shammai (the House of Shammai). In almost every one of these disputes, Hillel's view prevailed. Rabbi Hillel was born to a wealthy family in Babylonia, but came to Jerusalem without the financial support of his family and supported himself as a woodcutter. It is said that he lived in such great poverty that he was sometimes unable to pay the admission fee to study Torah, and because of him that fee was abolished. He was known for his kindness, his gentleness, and his concern for humanity. One of his most famous sayings, recorded in Pirkei Avot (Ethics of the Fathers, a tractate of the Mishnah), is "If I am not for myself, then who will be for me? And if I am only for myself, then what am I? And if not now, when?" The Hillel organization, a network of Jewish college student organizations, is named for him. Rabbi Shammai was an engineer, known for the strictness of his views. He was reputed to be dour, quick-tempered and impatient. For example, the Talmud tells that a gentile came to Shammai saying that he would convert to Judaism if Shammai could teach him the whole Torah in the time that he could stand on one foot. Shammai drove him away with a builder's measuring stick! Hillel, on the other hand, converted the gentile by telling him, "That which is hateful to you, do not do to your neighbor. That is the whole Torah; the rest is commentary. Hillel and Shammai- Jewish Virtual Library, Copyright *American-Israeli Cooperative Enterprise*, Reprinted with permission.

they could never marry each other again. The reason for this restriction is difficult to determine. One widely accepted explanation is that it would make a husband think carefully before divorcing his wife and marrying another woman.

In summary, while we have no record of the occasion when, God led Moses to make it possible for the men in Israel to divorce their wives, Jesus made it clear that it happened. He declared that Moses did this "because of the hardness of your hearts" (Mt. 19:8). Callous-hearted men would commit greater evils against wives who were despised in their eyes if divorce were not an option. As noted earlier, God had already forbidden the sale of a wife into slavery. But a hard-hearted man in a male-dominated society could find many other ways to make life difficult for a wife he no longer wanted to support. He could displease her by marrying and lavishing all his attention on a second wife. He could burden her with too much work while openly resenting her continued presence. He would be limited only by his own imagination and vindictiveness.

Chapter 3

The Divine Guidance

Now it came to pass, when Jesus had finished these sayings, *that* He departed from Galilee and came to the region of Judea beyond the Jordan. And great multitudes followed Him, and He healed them there. The Pharisees also came to Him, testing Him, and saying to Him, "Is it lawful for a man to divorce his wife for *just* any reason?" And He answered and said to them, "Have you not read that He who made *them* at the beginning *'made them male and female,'* and said, *'For this reason a man shall leave his father and mother and be joined to his wife, and the two shall become one flesh?'* So then, they are no longer two but one flesh. Therefore what God has joined together, let not man separate." They said to Him, "Why then did Moses command to give a certificate of divorce, and to put her away?" He said to them, "Moses, because of the hardness of your hearts, permitted you to divorce your wives, but from the beginning it was not so. And I say to you, whoever divorces his wife, except for sexual immorality, and marries another, commits adultery; and whoever marries her who is divorced commits adultery." His disciples said to Him, "If such is the case of the man with *his* wife, it is better not to marry." -Matthew 19:1-10

This is the second key passage on the divorce issue. It expresses our Lord's teaching on this subject more fully than any other Gospel passage.

The Historical Situation

As noted earlier, the religious leaders among the Jews disagreed sharply on the divorce issue. The followers of Rabbi Shammai were far stricter than the followers of Rabbi Hillel. The enemies of Jesus asked Him, "Can a man divorce his wife for any reason?" hoping they could force Him into giving an answer that would put Him at odds with one group or the other. Jesus didn't fall into their trap. He corrected their statement that Moses *commanded* men to divorce their wives by reminding them that Moses *permitted* divorce because of the hard hearts of the men. He also called them back to God's ideal before making a pronouncement that agreed with the teaching of neither of the prominent rabbinical schools.

The Provision Made

Jesus said that divorce is wrong "except for sexual immorality." The Greek word He used was *porneia*[11], a term covering a wide range of sexual sins[12]. When used in

[11] *Strong's Hebrew and Greek Dictionaries:* G4202 porneia From G4203; *harlotry* (including *adultery* and *incest*); figuratively *idolatry:*—fornication.

[12]Walvoord, John, Roy Zuck, *The Bible Knowledge Commentary.* Ontario, Victor Books, 1983, p63. Bible scholars differ over the meaning of this "exception clause," found only in Matthew's Gospel. The word for "marital unfaithfulness" is *porneiaö*

(1) Some feel Jesus used this as a synonym for adultery (*moicheia*). Therefore adultery by either partner in a marriage is the only sufficient grounds for a marriage to end in divorce. Among those holding this view, some believe remarriage is possible but others believe remarriage should never occur.

(2) Others define *porneia* as a sexual offense that could occur only in the betrothal period when a Jewish man and woman were considered married but had not yet consummated their coming marriage with sexual intercourse. If in this

a sentence alongside *moicheia*[13] (adultery), it denoted a sexual sin involving at least one unmarried person or a perverted form of sexual behavior. The feminine form of this word *porne* means "prostitute." The masculine *pornos* denoted either a man who was promiscuous or who engaged in perverted sexual behavior. On rare occasions, when specified by the context, it referred to a marriage of close relatives. Therefore, all the modern versions render the word *porneia* here as either "unchastity," "unfaithfulness," or "sexual immorality."

In sanctioning divorce for sexual immorality, Jesus also permitted remarriage for people thus divorced. A careful study of the Biblical passages dealing with divorce makes clear a principle that we can apply. Whenever a divorce occurs on grounds God has declared valid, that divorce carries with it the right of remarriage. We can express this principle with confidence on the basis of the historical situation into which Jesus spoke these words and on the grammar of the words themselves.

period the woman was found pregnant (as was Mary; Matt. 1:18-19), a divorce could occur in order to break the contract.

(3) Still others believe the term *porneia* referred to illegitimate marriages within prohibited degrees of kinship, as in Leviticus 18:6-18. If a man discovered that his wife was a near relative, he would actually be involved in an incestuous marriage. Then this would be a justifiable grounds for divorce. Some say this meaning of *porneia* is found in Acts 15:20, 29 (cf. 1 Cor. 5:1).

(4) Another view is that *porneia* refers to a relentless, persistent, unrepentant lifestyle of sexual unfaithfulness (different from a one-time act of illicit relations). (In the NT *porneia* is broader than *moicheia*). Such a continued practice would thus be the basis for divorce, since such unfaithful and unrelenting conduct would have broken the marriage bond.

[13] *Strong's Hebrew and Greek Dictionaries:* G3429 μοιχάω moichaō From G3432; (middle voice) to *commit adultery:*—commit adultery.

First, let's place ourselves in the shoes of those to whom Jesus spoke. The Jews in His audience, whether followers of Hillel or Shammai, agreed that legally divorced people had the right to marry new mates. As far as we know, no Jewish teachers of that time differed on this point. We can therefore assume that the people Jesus addressed had never heard of a divorce that did not carry with it the right to remarry. The divorce regulations mentioned in Deuteronomy 24:1-4 completely dissolved prior marital commitments. The only prohibition was that a divorced couple not remarry each other after marrying and divorcing new mates.

The second basis for our conviction that a God-permitted divorce carries with it the right to remarry is found in the very words recorded in Matthew 19:9, "Whoever divorces his wife, except for sexual immorality, and marries another, commits adultery." The phrase "except for sexual immorality" appears in the middle of the sentence. But the meaning would be the same if it appeared at the beginning of the sentence. "Except for sexual immorality, whoever divorces his wife and marries another commits adultery." It would be the same if it read, "Whoever divorces his wife and marries another commits adultery, except for sexual immorality." An exceptive clause grammatically applies to the whole sentence, whether it appears at the beginning, in the middle, or at the end.

Dr. A.T. Robertson further explains the exception clause in the passage:

> Except for fornication (*parektos logou porneias*). This is the marginal reading in Westcott and Hort which also adds "maketh her an adulteress" (*poiei auten moicheutheaith*) and also these words: "and he that marrieth her when she is put away committeth adultery" (*kai ho apolelumenen gamesas moichatai*). There seems to be a certain amount of assimilation in various manuscripts between this verse and the words in 5:32. But, whatever reading is accepted here, even the short one in Westcott and Hort (*me epi porneiai*, not for fornication), it is plain that Matthew represents Jesus in both places as allowing divorce for fornication as a general term (*porneia*) which is technically adultery (*moicheia* from *moichaō or moicheuō*). Here, as in 5:31f., a group of scholars deny the genuineness of the exception given by Matthew alone. McNeile holds that "the

addition of the saving clause is, in fact, opposed to the spirit of the whole context, and must have been made at a time when the practice of divorce for adultery had already grown up." That in my opinion is gratuitous criticism, which is unwilling to accept Matthew's report because it disagrees with one's views on the subject of divorce. He adds: "It cannot be supposed that Matthew wished to represent Jesus as siding with the school of Shammai." Why not, if Shammai on this point agreed with Jesus? Those who deny Matthew's report are those who are opposed to remarriage at all. Jesus by implication, as in 5:31, does allow remarriage of the innocent party, but not of the guilty one. Certainly Jesus has lifted the whole subject of marriage and divorce to a new level, far beyond the petty contentions of the schools of Hillel and Shammai.[14]

The idea that God permitted divorce for sexual immorality but forbade remarriage arose in the post-apostolic era when some of the Church Fathers began to view human sexuality as a necessary evil and exalted celibacy as the most God-honoring lifestyle. Not only did

---

[14] Robertson, A.T., *Word Pictures of the New Testament,* "Matthew"

they discourage marriage, they forbade remarriage either after a divorce or the death of a spouse.

We conclude, therefore, that Jesus permitted divorce on grounds of sexual immorality, and that this divorce assumed the right of remarriage.

As Dr. J. Vernon Mcgee put it,

> Because of the hardness of the human heart, God permitted divorce. God is merciful to us—oh, how merciful! But His ideal is never divorce. I recognize that we are living in a culture, which is very lax in this area. There are multitudes of divorced folk who will be reading this book. Let me repeat that the background of divorce is always sin. But, after all, all of us are sinners. Since God can forgive murderers, He can also forgive divorced folk, *even if remarried*. But we need to recognize that the root cause of divorce is sin.[15]

The Restriction Imposed

The words of Jesus, "except for sexual immorality," express a restriction as well as a permission. If a person

---

[15]McGee, J. Vernon, *Thru the Bible with J. Vernon McGee*, Nashville: Thomas Nelson Publishers 2000, 1981.

obtains a divorce on grounds other than sexual immorality and remarries, he commits adultery. The Lord's use of the word *moicheia* rather than *porneia* is significant. *Moicheia* focuses on the broken marriage covenant. When two people whose divorces were not valid in God's sight come together in the sexual union of marriage, they break their former marriage covenant. But this is not a continuing state. From this point on they are husband and wife.

God considers two people as married when they have met the civil requirements. This is true even when their divorces were not valid in God's sight. Jesus told the Samaritan woman that she had five husbands before her present live-in arrangement:

> The woman answered and said, "I have no husband." Jesus said to her, "You have well said, 'I have no husband,' for you have had five husbands, and the one whom you now have is not your husband; in that you spoke truly." -Jn. 4:17-18

It is unlikely that she was widowed five times. We can therefore assume that at least a couple of her marriages followed a divorce. Jesus still recognized each man she married as a husband.

Moreover, in 1 Corinthians 7:20 Paul urged first-century believers to do their best to remain in the marriage they had when they were converted. The people he addressed must have included some who had married new mates after divorces obtained on trivial grounds. If these people were living in perpetual adultery, we can assume that Paul would have told them to separate immediately.

This leads us to the conclusion that when two people marry after a divorce on grounds less than specified by Jesus and Paul, they sin against the covenant they made in the previous marriage. But this occurs only once. Their first sexual union breaks the former bond. The new marriage covenant is now in effect. This fact, however, should not be taken as weakening the force of Christ's restriction. Deliberate disobedience is always a serious matter. Believers who truly love the Lord will not lightly ignore or disobey Him.

Chapter 4

THE DIVINE GUIDANCE

Now to the married I command, yet not I but the Lord: A wife is not to depart from her husband. But even if she does depart, let her remain unmarried or be reconciled to her husband. And a husband is not to divorce his wife. But to the rest I, not the Lord, say: If any brother has a wife who does not believe, and she is willing to live with him, let him not divorce her. And a woman who has a husband who does not believe, if he is willing to live with her, let her not divorce him. For the unbelieving husband is sanctified by the wife, and the unbelieving wife is sanctified by the husband; otherwise your children would be unclean, but now they are holy. But if the unbeliever departs, let him depart; a brother or a sister is not under bondage in such cases. But God has called us to peace. For how do you know, O wife, whether you will save your husband? Or how do you know, O husband, whether you will save your wife? -1 Corinthians 7:10-16

Apart from a passing comment in Romans 7[16], these few verses contain everything Paul wrote about divorce. Some critics say that in the process he contradicted Jesus' stipulation that the only grounds for divorce was sexual immorality. But a careful consideration of the historical circumstances makes it clear that Paul was faithful to Jesus' words on this matter.

---

[16] Romans 7:1-4 Or do you not know, brethren (for I speak to those who know the law), that the law has dominion over a man as long as he lives? For the woman who has a husband is bound by the law to *her* husband as long as he lives. But if the husband dies, she is released from the law of *her* husband. So then if, while *her* husband lives, she marries another man, she will be called an adulteress; but if her husband dies, she is free from that law, so that she is no adulteress, though she has married another man.

The Historical Situation

When Jesus made His statements about divorce, He addressed Jewish people living under the Mosaic law. Paul addressed believers, both Jews and Gentiles, on this side of Calvary and the empty tomb. Many of these Gentile believers undoubtedly came out of a paganism that was morally decadent. Pagan worship involved temple prostitution and sexual orgies. The city of Corinth itself was known far and wide as a center of sexual indulgence and other forms of immorality[17].

The pagans who became Christians needed often to be reminded of God's moral standards. Then too, some of those who had become believers were living with a mate who had not become a Christian. Apparently, a number of the non-Christian spouses were content to allow the marriage to remain intact. Other nonbelievers, however, wanted the mate either to renounce Christ or to end the marriage.

Paul was concerned that fellow believers be as unencumbered as possible from the normal cares of life so they could serve Christ freely in the difficult days that were ahead. Therefore, in chapter 7 of his first epistle to the Corinthians he gave inspired advice and instruction about singleness, marriage, divorce, and remarriage. We

[17] Douglas, J.D., Merrill C. Tenney, *The New International Dictionary of the Bible*, Winona Lake, BMH, 1987, p.233-235

will consider only the verses that deal directly with the divorce and remarriage problems.

The Provision Made

Paul advised single people to remain single, and married people to remain with their present mate. However, he declared that the unmarried would not sin by marrying a believer and that a Christian with a non-Christian mate who wanted out of the marriage would not sin by allowing the unbeliever to obtain a divorce.

> But if the unbeliever departs, let him depart; a brother or a sister is not under bondage in such cases. *(The word Paul used here was the official term for "divorce" on the legal certificates of that day)*-1 Cor. 7:15

The fact that Paul made the desertion of a believer by an unbeliever grounds for divorce, while Jesus gave the only valid reason as "sexual immorality," does not put him into conflict with his Master. He was addressing a different situation, a mixed marriage. Jesus, addressing Jews under the law, had in mind marriages between Jews, marriages within the covenant community. Paul confronted a different problem, marriages between believers and nonbelievers.

God through the apostle Paul declared that a believer does not sin by allowing a divorce when the unbeliever wants out. A divorce in such circumstances is therefore valid. God sees the marriage as ended. Therefore, the believer thus divorced has the right to remarry.

From the words of Jesus in Matthew 19 and from Paul in 1 Corinthians 7:15, we have found only two grounds upon which God sanctions divorce: *sexual immorality* and the *desertion of a believer by an unbeliever.* This raises the question, "Is divorce wrong under all other circumstances? What about abuse? Must a woman continue to live with a man who is beating her and sexually abusing her?"

There is no verse in the Bible specifically stating that a woman in an abusive marriage has a right to obtain a divorce. Nor is there any mention of a legal separation. Many pastors and other Christian leaders have gone through great emotional and mental turmoil when confronted with extreme cruelty situations. And in studying the Scriptures I have found a principle that I believe we can apply in such situations. It permits some women to seek a divorce even when the husband was a professing Christian and free from sexual immorality. Let me explain.

God in His compassion sometimes allows His people to set aside strict conformity to certain rules He has given. He did this on one occasion when David and his men were hungry. He allowed them to eat consecrated bread in the tabernacle, bread, which He had declared holy:

> Now David came to Nob, to Ahimelech the priest. And Ahimelech was afraid when he met David, and said to him, "Why are you alone, and no one is with you?"

> So David said to Ahimelech the priest, "The king has ordered me on some business, and said to me, 'Do not let anyone know anything about the business on which I send you, or what I have commanded you.' And I have directed my young men to such and such a place. Now therefore, what have you on hand? Give me five loaves of bread in my hand, or whatever can be found."

> And the priest answered David and said, "There is no common bread on hand; but there is holy bread, if the young men have at least kept themselves from women."

> Then David answered the priest, and said to him, "Truly, women have been kept from us about three days since I came out. And the vessels of the young men are holy, and the bread is in effect common, even though it was consecrated in the vessel this day."

So the priest gave him holy bread; for there was no bread there but the showbread which had been taken from before the LORD, in order to put hot bread in its place on the day when it was taken away. -1 Sam. 21:1-6

God also did this with His Sabbath rules. He had commanded the Israelites to keep the seventh day as a day of absolute rest-even for domestic animals (Ex. 20:8-11). He forbade the kindling of a fire to cook food (Ex. 35:1-3). The importance of these rules was seen when He ordered that a man be stoned for gathering sticks on the Sabbath (Num. 15:32-36). It was to be a day of absolute rest!

Yet Jesus healed on the Sabbath. When rebuked by His adversaries, He reminded them that even a legalistic Jew worked to free an animal that had fallen into a pit:

Now when He had departed from there, He went into their synagogue. And behold, there was a man who had a withered hand. And they asked Him, saying, "Is it lawful to heal on the Sabbath?"—that they might accuse Him.

Then He said to them, "What man is there among you who has one sheep, and if

it falls into a pit on the Sabbath, will not lay
hold of it and lift it out? Of how much more
value then is a man than a sheep? Therefore
it is lawful to do good on the Sabbath." Then
He said to the man, "Stretch out your hand."
And he stretched it out, and it was restored
as whole as the other. -Mt. 12:9-13

The strong "no work" regulation could be set aside
when an animal needed help or a person needed healing.
The Bible doesn't say this explicitly, but the Jews knew it
to be true. The Lord Jesus expressed this fact when He
said, "The Sabbath was made for man, and not man for the
Sabbath" (Mk. 2:27).

Let us apply this principle to God's regulations about
divorce. Why did God give men permission to divorce
their wives? Jesus answered this question when He told
His critics, "because of the hardness of your hearts" (Mt.
19:8). God had declared that a man should cleave to his
wife in a one-flesh relationship (Gen. 2:24). He never
rescinded this rule. Yet He permitted men to divorce their
wives. Why? The only logical reason we can see is that
He did so to protect the wives of hard-hearted men. If a
man didn't want a woman as a wife any longer, he couldn't
just discard her, he had to give her a certificate of divorce.
This would give her the freedom to marry another man.
The Old Testament divorce laws were a merciful

provision. God hated divorce then just as He does now. But He preferred divorce to the abuse of wives and mothers.

Divorce is often a terrible evil, but in some situations it represents a wise and loving course of action. Ezra insisted that Israelite men put away their pagan wives and children (Ezra 10:10-19). God Himself divorced the northern tribes of Israel (Jer. 3:8). He took such action only after enduring their prolonged spiritual unfaithfulness, which He compared to sexual unfaithfulness.

Since divorce is not always wrong, it is not like lying, stealing, coveting, or sexual immorality. These other actions are always wrong. God can never approve of them. But divorce is not always a sin. It is always caused by sin, but is not an act of disobedience when permitted by God.

Believers are not necessarily sinning when they divorce a spouse who through sexual sin has shattered the exclusive commitment of the marriage covenant. In fact, a woman who is married to a physically abusive husband may not be sinning when, with the encouragement of her spiritual counselors, she seeks divorce even if her husband is not guilty of sexual immorality. If such a wife has given careful consideration to the name and reputation of Christ, if she has sought to fulfill the requirements of love, and if she has followed the biblical procedures for confronting a sinning brother...

Moreover if your brother sins against you, go and tell him his fault between you and him alone. If he hears you, you have gained your brother. But if he will not hear, take with you one or two more, that *'by the mouth of two or three witnesses every word may be established.'* And if he refuses to hear them, tell *it* to the church. But if he refuses even to hear the church, let him be to you like a heathen and a tax collector. -Mt. 18:15-17

...then she may have reason to seek divorce against someone who is no longer being treated by the church as a brother.

As noted earlier, Jesus taught that sometimes the spirit of the law allows specific legal requirements to be overridden (Mt. 12:1-13). By His own example, Jesus allowed His hungry disciples to pick and eat grain on the Sabbath, just as He also took the opportunity to heal a man with a crippled hand on a day when no work was to be done.

I believe the apostle Paul could have had this same spirit of the law in mind when he wrote:

Now to the married I command, yet not I but the Lord: A wife is not to depart from

her husband. But even if she does depart, let
her remain unmarried or be reconciled to her
husband. And a husband is not to divorce his
wife. -1 Cor. 7:10-11

Notice that after commanding the Christian wife not to
divorce her husband, the apostle inserted, "But even if she
does depart, let her remain unmarried or be reconciled to
her husband." Why didn't he just tell both husbands and
wives to refrain from divorcing one another without
inserting "but even if she does"? I believe that Paul may
have been making a compassionate provision for an
abused woman.

The Restriction Imposed

Paul told the woman, who obtained a divorce on
grounds other than sexual immorality, that she was to
"remain unmarried or be reconciled to her husband." Such
a divorce is not as complete a severing of the marriage
bond as one where a mate has been guilty of sexual
immorality or where an unbeliever refuses to continue
living with a believer. To enter a new marriage while the
possibility of reconciliation is still open is to commit
adultery, as specified in Matthew 19:9. It seems logical to
assume that once one of the parties makes remarriage
impossible by entering a new union, the other party is

released from this requirement just as if the former mate had died.

I realize that there is an element of subjectivity in determining when principles of wisdom and love call for a divorce under such conditions. But we make such decisions all the time in all areas of life.

What is important is that our personal judgment be guided by the right principles. Any exception to the "law" should be considered only in light of the most basic principles of Scripture. We cannot be justified in a divorce action if we have not first considered what effect our actions will have on the name and reputation of the One whose name we bear. Is this action being taken to please the Lord?

> But this I say, brethren, the time *is* short, so that from now on even those who have wives should be as though they had none, those who weep as though they did not weep, those who rejoice as though they did not rejoice, those who buy as though they did not possess, and those who use this world as not misusing *it*. For the form of this world is passing away.
>
> But I want you to be without care. He who is unmarried cares for the things of the Lord—how he may please the Lord. But he

who is married cares about the things of the world—how he may please his wife. There is a difference between a wife and a virgin. The unmarried woman cares about the things of the Lord, that she may be holy both in body and in spirit. But she who is married cares about the things of the world—how she may please her husband. And this I say for your own profit, not that I may put a leash on you, but for what is proper, and that you may serve the Lord without distraction. -1 Cor. 7:29-35

Is the motive for the action godly? Is the action being considered only for a person's own self-protection, or also for the good of the sinning mate? (1 Cor. 13:1-3). Has the sinned-against spouse sought safety in the advice of wise counselors? (Prov. 11:14). Has the one considering divorce carefully weighed the implications of two Christians pleading their dispute before a civil judge or jury? (1 Cor. 6:1-7). Is divorce a last-resort action taken with the support of wise counsel, when the other party can no longer be treated as a follower of Christ? All of this and more is necessary to assure that persons who are taking exception to their marriage vows, and to the binding law of marriage, are doing so according to the proper biblical procedure.

Chapter 5

THE PROPER PROCEDURE

When nonbelievers decide to get a divorce, they can go directly to the civil authorities and take action. Not so for Christians! In the first place, we must think of 1 Corinthians 6:1-8.

> Dare any of you, having a matter against another, go to law before the unrighteous, and not before the saints? Do you not know that the saints will judge the world? And if the world will be judged by you, are you unworthy to judge the smallest matters? Do

you not know that we shall judge angels? How much more, things that pertain to this life? If then you have judgments concerning things pertaining to this life, do you appoint those who are least esteemed by the church to judge? I say this to your shame. Is it so, that there is not a wise man among you, not even one, who will be able to judge between his brethren? But brother goes to law against brother, and that before unbelievers! Now therefore, it is already an utter failure for you that you go to law against one another. Why do you not rather accept wrong? Why do you not rather *let yourselves* be cheated? No, you yourselves do wrong and cheat, and *you do* these things *to your* brethren!

Paul said that we dishonor Christ before the unbelieving world when we go to court against a fellow believer.

Second, the love principle calls on us to seek the spiritual good of fallen Christians, no matter what they have done. Then too, a believer should think very carefully before breaking the "for better or for worse as long as we both shall live" marriage vow. After failing on their own to get the attention of their mate, wronged or hurting Christians can take steps to increase pressure on the offending spouse by asking one or two others to act as witnesses to the problem. This procedure was outlined by Jesus and recorded in Matthew 18:15-21.

"Moreover if your brother sins against you, go and tell him his fault between you and him alone. If he hears you, you have gained your brother. But if he will not hear, take with you one or two more, that *'by the mouth of two or three witnesses every word may be established.'* And if he refuses to hear them, tell *it* to the church. But if he refuses even to hear the church, let him be to you like a heathen and a tax collector.

"Assuredly, I say to you, whatever you bind on earth will be bound in heaven, and whatever you loose on earth will be loosed in heaven.

"Again I say to you that if two of you agree on earth concerning anything that they ask, it will be done for them by My Father in heaven. For where two or three are gathered together in My name, I am there in the midst of them."

> Then Peter came to Him and said, "Lord,
> how often shall my brother sin against me,
> and I forgive him? Up to seven times?"

Such confrontation, however, does not always work. The next step is to ask the church to use its influence in seeking to bring about a change of heart. If the offending mate still doesn't respond, then the church must formally disassociate itself from the sinning member. Paul gave us an example of this when he told the church in Corinth to excommunicate a man who was living in an incestuous relationship (1 Cor. 5:4-5).

> In the name of our Lord Jesus Christ,
> when you are gathered together, along with
> my spirit, with the power of our Lord Jesus
> Christ, deliver such a one to Satan for the
> destruction of the flesh, that his spirit may
> be saved in the day of the Lord Jesus.

After much prayer and serious effort to lead the sinning person to repentance has failed and the excommunication process has been carried out, the wrongdoer is to be treated "like a heathen and a tax gatherer" (Mt. 18:17). The person may be a genuine believer, but he is now looked upon as an unbeliever. This means that though we still love him and desire his spiritual restoration, we can now go to a secular court for a divorce. Even then, the wronged believers must be careful about their testimony. It should be apparent to the judge and all other observers that the innocent mate is not a greedy or vindictive person. We must always keep in mind our Lord's exhortations to go the extra mile (Mt. 5:41) and to love our enemies (Mt. 5:43-44). Remember too that the apostle Paul declared that we should be willing to be cheated rather than to bring reproach on Jesus Christ (1 Cor. 6:7).

This biblical procedure cannot be followed completely if the erring spouse is not a church member. But even then, wronged persons can seek counsel, exercise patience, and be conscious of their testimony when reaching a settlement.

Chapter 6

THE GOD-HONORING GOAL

The apostle Paul told us that we are to do everything to the glory of God (1 Cor. 10:31). This should be our goal, even when considering a divorce. In such a situation we glorify God by doing all we can to protect the name of Christ from reproach and by seeking the eternal good of everyone involved-including the offender.

A divorce between Christians tends to reflect badly on the Lord Jesus. It can be viewed by nonbelievers as an indication that faith in Christ is not as life changing as we proclaim it to be. Even after church discipline has given believers the authority to deal with the sinning mate as an unsaved person, the people in the court and the public will view both parties as believers. It seems to me that the Christian who has been wronged should be fair, even to the point of being overly generous. A bitter court fight should be avoided if at all possible.

> Now therefore, it is already an utter failure for you that you go to law against one another. Why do you not rather accept wrong? Why do you not rather *let yourselves* be cheated? -1 Cor. 6:7

We also glorify God by showing love for the offenders. We can do this by treating them kindly, by doing our best to lead them to repent, and by forgiving them when they do. These repentant offenders should feel the warmth of our love.

After they have given good reason for the church to believe in the reality of their repentance, they should be restored to fellowship. The apostle Paul had to address this situation in 2 Corinthians because the congregation was apparently withholding restoration to the man who had been excommunicated for an incestuous relationship (1 Cor. 5:4-5). In 2 Corinthians 2:5-11 he wrote:

> If anyone has caused grief, he has not grieved me, but all of you to some extent-

not to be too severe. This punishment which was inflicted by the majority is sufficient for such a man, so that, on the contrary, you ought rather to forgive and comfort him, lest perhaps such a one be swallowed up with too much sorrow. Therefore I urge you to reaffirm your love to him. . . . Now whom you forgive anything, I also forgive. For if indeed I have forgiven anything, I have forgiven that one for your sakes in the presence of Christ, lest Satan should take advantage of us; for we are not ignorant of his devices.

Those who repent should also gradually be restored to places of service. The time frame and the degree of the restoration must be determined case by case. It is almost impossible to set up a rigid timetable procedure. The situation is quite similar to that of restoring a pastor who has fallen into sexual immorality. Sometimes full restoration is possible; sometimes it is unwise. After immoral conduct or an unwarranted divorce, we must be keenly aware of Paul's requirement that a church leader be "blameless" and "have a good testimony among them who are outside" (1 Tim. 3:2,7).

One mistake often made is that divorce is viewed as the sin of all sins. Men who repent of sexual immorality are often restored to service far more readily than those who wrongly obtain a divorce. I have heard of Christian workers who had been guilty of sexual immorality restored to their offices, while innocent victims of an unfaithful mate were rejected.

A former pastor I know lost his position in a Christian organization when his wife left him and married another man. She admitted that he had been a good husband and father, but said his income level had been too low. He now is not permitted to serve as an elder because he is viewed as not meeting the "husband of one wife" requirement of 1 Timothy 3:2. This man, an innocent victim of his wife's greed, had been dealt with far more severely than many pastors who repented after immorality. This troubles me. A man thus divorced still meets the "husband of one wife" qualification, even after a new marriage. The Greek expression is literally "a one-woman man.[18]" This refers to a man whose life as a husband was marked by fidelity to his mate. A good husband who remarries after his wife dies is also a "one-woman man" in spite of having a second wife.

We must therefore recognize that God sometimes permits divorce. Since this is true, a person does not sin when he or she obtains a divorce on grounds of sexual

---

[18] Robertson, A.T., *Word Pictures of the New Testament*, 1 Tim: "μιας γυναιας ανδρα: Of one woman (*mias gunaikos*). One at a time, clearly."

immorality or desertion by an unsaved spouse. Let's not treat such people as somehow and somewhat tainted!

People who have divorced on inadequate grounds and remarry have sinned. But their sin is just as forgivable as any other sin. A person who has been wrongly divorced and remarried but has repented should be treated no different than someone who has repented of any other sin. We are to forgive all who repent. And we must seek their restoration to usefulness in the Lord's service.

Restoration to leadership such as with a deacon, elder, pastor, or a Bible teacher is to be handled with much care. In 1 Timothy 3:1-7, the apostle Paul placed much emphasis on making sure that the prospective elders and deacons be "blameless" and have a "good reputation on the outside." When Christian leaders obtain a divorce and remarry, a group of Spirit-filled believers should work with them. Sometimes these church appointed people may be led to grant full restoration; sometimes not. The wrongdoer, realizing that the name and reputation of Christ is at stake, should humbly accept their decision.

In summary, the Bible permits divorce and remarriage on two grounds: sexual infidelity and the desertion of a believer by an unbeliever. However, a Christian should never rush into divorce, no matter what the situation. Sincere effort must be made to bring the wrongdoer to repentance. Spirit-filled men and women should be involved with the wronged spouse to reach this goal. If the sinning party is a church member, the discipline procedure of Matthew 18 must be carried out. If not, fellow believers can offer counsel and be involved in supportive prayer. People who disobeyed God in their divorce and remarriage must be shown love, even though we do not approve of what they did. The aim should be their repentance and restoration to fellowship. Restoration, especially to that of leadership, must be handled very carefully to protect the name and reputation of Christ.

Chapter 7

SPIRITUALLY EQUIPPED

Living up to what the Bible teaches about sexual morality, marriage, and divorce is very demanding. Abstinence before marriage is out of style in our society. So is submission for the wife and self-sacrificing love on the part of the husband. The idea that believers should remain unmarried if they obtain a divorce on grounds less than sexual infidelity or desertion by an unbeliever is scoffed at or ignored. These ideals are attainable, but in today's world it is more difficult than ever to do so.

On the other hand we are quick to judge anyone who is experiencing a divorce as worse than an infidel. There is no other sin that weighs so heavily on the church as divorce. One might say that it is the last "unforgivable sin." Regardless of the circumstances, whether infidelity, abandonment or even abuse, those who are divorced are outcasts. I recently heard of a case of a single mother being driven away from a church that she had come to for comfort. She was called a harlot and told to never come back. This is shameful. Remember, Jesus sat with prostitutes and tax collectors in order to reach them with the gospel.

On the other side of the coin, we are challenged to be sympathetic, accepting, and forgiving toward divorced people, even to the point of fully restoring those who repent.

If we have these feelings, we need to join Paul in praying that we, "being rooted and grounded in love, may be able to comprehend . . . what is the width and length and depth and height, to know the love of Christ which passes knowledge; that [we] may be filled with all the fullness of God" (Eph. 3:17-19). When God answers this prayer, we will be amazed at His love. And through the indwelling Holy Spirit, we will want to live up to God's expectations for us and be eager to forgive and accept those who have stumbled and fallen.

APPENDIX

Word study of ἀπολύω

There are 11 occurrences of the verb form of this word in the New Testament. Each of them are produced and discussed below.

Matthew 1:19	Then Joseph her husband, being a just *man,* and not wanting to make her a public example, was minded to put her away secretly.	*Joseph had reason to suspect infidelity as Mary was pregnant before they were actually married*
15:32	Now Jesus called His disciples to *Himself* and said, "I have compassion on the multitude, because they have now continued with Me three days and have nothing to eat. And I do not want to send them away hungry, lest they faint on the way."	*In the context Jesus did not want to send the crowd away with nothing to eat.*

19:3	The Pharisees also came to Him, testing Him, and saying to Him, "Is it lawful for a man to divorce his wife for *just* any reason?"	*Here the Pharisees were trying to trap Jesus, by causing Him to contradict the Law. Here the traditional meaning of "divorce" is the meaning of the word.*
19:7	They said to Him, "Why then did Moses command to give a certificate of divorce, and to put her away?"	
19:8	He said to them, "Moses, because of the hardness of your hearts, permitted you to divorce your wives, but from the beginning it was not so."	*Divorce was permitted as a demonstration of God's mercy towards those who could not defend themselves.*
Mark 10:2	The Pharisees came and asked Him, "Is it lawful	

	for a man to divorce *his* wife?" testing Him.	
10:4	They said, "Moses permitted *a man* to write a certificate of divorce, and to dismiss *her.*"	
Luke 23:20	Pilate, therefore, wishing to release Jesus, again called out to them. But they shouted, saying, "Crucify *Him,* crucify Him!"	*Here Pilate wanted to "release" Jesus from the penalty of the law. Notice the continuity of the idea along side the idea of divorce.*
John 19:10	Then Pilate said to Him, "Are You not speaking to me? Do You not know that I have power to crucify You, and power to release You?"	
19:12	From then on Pilate sought to release Him, but the Jews cried out, saying, "If you let this	

	Man go, you are not Caesar's friend. Whoever makes himself a king speaks against Caesar."	
Acts 28:18	who, when they had examined me, wanted to let me go, because there was no cause for putting me to death	*Here Paul uses the word in context of being "let go" or released from the penalty of the law.*

Dictionary entry: ἀπολύω

release, set free; send away; send off; divorce; forgive; middle leave (Acts 28:25)

Word study of ἀποστάσιον

There are 3 occurrences of the noun form of this word in the New Testament. Each of them are produced and discussed below.

Matthew 5:31	"Furthermore it has been said, 'Whoever divorces his wife, let him give her a certificate of divorce.	*Here the word is used of the official document concerning the divorce.*
19:7	They said to Him, "Why then did Moses command to give a certificate of divorce, and to put her away?"	
Mark 10:4	They said, "Moses permitted *a man* to write a certificate of divorce, and to dismiss *her.*"	
Dictionary entry: ἀποστάσιον, ου neuter (with or without βιβλίον) *written notice of divorce*		

Word study of ἀφίημι

There are 3 occurrences of this word in the New Testament. Each of them are produced and discussed below.

1 Corinthians 7:11	But even if she does depart, let her remain unmarried or be reconciled to *her* husband. And a husband is not to divorce *his* wife.	*This word carries with it the authority to allow one to depart.*
7:12	But to the rest I, not the Lord, say: If any brother has a wife who does not believe, and she is willing to live with him, let him not divorce her.	
7:13	And a woman who has a husband who does not believe, if he is willing to live with her, let her not divorce him.	
Dictionary entry: ἀφίημι		

cancel; *forgive, remit* (of sin or debts); *allow, let be, tolerate* (ἄφες ἴδωμεν *Wait! Let us see!* or simply *Let us see!* Mt 27:49; Mk 15:36); *leave; leave behind, forsake, neglect; let go, dismiss, divorce;* ἀφῆκεν τό πνεῦμα *he died* (Mt 27:50); ἀ. φωνήν μεγάλην *give a loud cry* (Mk 15:37)

GENERAL INDEX

SCRIPTURE INDEX

BIBLIOGRAPHY

Adams, Jay E. *Marriage, Divorce, and Remarriage in the Bible.* Grand Rapids: Zondervan 1980

Adams, Jay E. *The Christian Counselor's Manual.* Grand Rapids: Zondervan 1973

Aland, Kurt. *The Greek New Testament with Dictionary.* Edmonds: United Bible Society 1966

Anderson, Ken. *Where to Find it in the Bible.* Nashville: Nelson 1996

Bartlett, Ross Allen. *Freedom from Emotional Bondage.* Spring Valley: The Trumpet Monthly Publication

Blomberg, Craig. *1 Corinthians.* Grand Rapids: Zondervan 1995

Brown, Francis and et al. *The Brown-Driver-Briggs Hebrew and English Lexicon.* Peabody: Hendrickson 1999

Cairns, Earle E. *Christianity through the Centuries.* Grand Rapids: Zondervan 1954

Chafer, Lewis Sperry. *He that is Spiritual.* Grand Rapids: Zondervan 1918

Chafer, Lewis Sperry. *Systematic Theology 1- 8 set.* Kregel

Clinebell, Howard. *Basic Types of Pastoral Care & Counseling.* Nashville: Abingdon 1966

Clinton, J. Robert. *The Making of a Leader.* Colorado Springs: Navpress 1988

Couch, Mal. *The Fundamentals for the Twenty-First Century.* Grand Rapids: Kregel 2000

Dana, H. E. and Julius R. Mantey. *A Manual Grammar of the Greek New Testament.* Upper Saddle River: Prentice Hall 1927

Davidson, Benjamin. *The Analytical Hebrew and Chaldee Lexicon.* Zondervan

Dobson, James C. *Love Must be Tough.* Dallas: Word 1983

Dobson, James C. *Marriage Counseling.* Ventura: Pehal book 1995

Edersheim, Alfred. *Bible History - Old Testament.* Peabody: Hendrickson 1995

Elliger, K. *Biblia Hebraica – Stuttgartensia.* Deutsche Biblegesellschaft 1969

Elwell, Walter A. *Evangelical Dictionary of Theology*. Cumbria: Baker 1984

Enns, Paul. *The Moody Handbook of Theology*. Chicago: Moody 1989

Freudenburg, Ben. *The Family Friendly Church*. Loveland: Vital ministry 1998

Geisler, Norman L. *A General Introduction to the Bible*. Chicago: Moody 1968

Geisler, Norman L. *Christian Apologetics*. Grand Rapids: Baker

Grassmick, John D. *Principles and Practice of Greek Exegesis* Dallas: Dallas Theological Seminary 1974

Grunlan, Stephen A. *Marriage and the Family*. Grand Rapids: Zondervan 1999

Harley, Willard F. *His Needs Her Needs*. Grand Rapids: Revell 1986

Hastings, James - Ed. *Hastings' Dictionary of the Bible*. New York: Hendrickson 1909

Hatch, Edwin and Hery A. Redpath. *Concordance to the Septuagint*. Grand Rapids: Baker 1897

Hodges, C. Zane. *The Greek New Testament According to the Majority Text*. Nashville: Nelson 1985

House, H. Wayne and Kenneth M. Durham. *Living Wisely in a Foolish World*. Grand Rapids: Kregel 1992

House, H. Wayne. *Divorce and Remarriage*. Downers Grove: IVP 1990

Hughes, R. Kent. *Disciplines of a Godly Man*. Wheaton: Crossway 1991

Kelley, Page H. *Biblical Hebrew*. Grand Rapids: Eerdmans 1992

Kent, Homer A. *Faith that Works*. Winona Lake: BMH Books 1986

Kent, Homer A. *The Pastoral Epistles (1 & 2 Timothy and Titus)*. Winona Lake: BMH Books 1986

Kubo, Sakae. *A Reader's Greek-English Lexicon of the New Testament*. Zondervan

Lightfoot, J. B. *Biblical Essays*. Hendrickson 1893

MacArthur, John F. *Introduction to Biblical Counseling*. Dallas: Word 1994

Mack, Wayne A. *Preparing for Marriage God's Way*. Tulsa: Virgil Hensley 1986

Mack, Wayne A. *Strengthening Your Marriage.* Phillipsburg: Presbyterian & Reformed 1997

Malphurs, Aubrey. *Maximizing Your Effectiveness.* Baker

Morley, Patrick. *Getting to Know the Man in the Mirror.* Nashville: Nelson 1994

O'Leary, K. Daniel and et al. *The Couples Psychotherapy.* New York: Wiley 1998

Perschbacher, Wesley J. *The New Analytical Greek Lexicon.* Peabody: Hendrickson 1990

Radmacher, Earl and et al - Eds. *New Illustrated Bible Commentary.* Nashville: Nelson 1999

Robertson, Archibald. *Word Pictures in the New Testament Set 1 – 6.* Broadman

Ryrie, Charles C. *Balancing the Christian Life.* Chicago: Moody 1969

Ryrie, Charles C. *Basic Theology.* Chicago: Moody 1986

Ryrie, Charles C. *The Holy Spirit.* Chicago: Moody 1965

Sanders, J. Oswald. *Spiritual Leadership.* Moody

Seamands, David A. *Healing for Damaged Emotions.* Wheaton: Victor 1981

Smalley, Gary. *Making Love Last Forever.* Dallas: Word 1996

Smith, Michael W. *She Said Yes.* Nashville: Word 1999

Solomon, Charles R. *Counseling with the Mind of Christ.* Old Tappan: Revell 1973

Southard, Samuel. *Theology & Therapy.* Dallas: Word 1989

Strong, James. *The New Strong's Exhaustive Concordance of the Bible.* Nashville: Nelson 1964

Unger, Merrill F. *The New Unger's Bible Dictionary.* Moody

Vine, W. E. *Vine's Complete Expository Dictionary.* Nashville: Nelson 1984

Vine, W. E. *Vine's Complete Expository Dictionary of Old & New Testament Words.* Nashville: Nelson 1984

Wallace, Daniel B. *Greek Grammar Beyond the Basics.* Grand Rapids: Zondervan 1996

Wallace, Daniel B. *The Basics of New Testament Syntax.* Grand Rapids: Zondervan 2000

Walvoord, John F. and Roy B. Zuck. *The Bible Knowledge Commentary (New Testament).* Colorado Springs: Victor 1983

Whiston, William. *The Works of Josephus.* Peabody: Hendrickson 1987

White, John. *Putting the Soul Back in Psychology.* Downers Grove: IVP 1987

Wiersbe, Warren W. *The Bible Exposition Commentary.* Colorado Springs: Victor 1989

Wiersbe, Warren W. *Wiersbe's Expository Outlines on the New Testament.* Colorado Springs:

Wiersbe, Warren W. *Wiersbe's Expository Outlines on the Old Testament.* Colorado Springs: Victor 1993

Wigram, George V. and Ralph D. Winter. *The Word Study New Testament and Concordance.* Wheaton: Wheaton 1972

Wynn, John C. *Family the Therapy in Pastoral ministry.* New York: Harpercollins 1982

Zodhiates, Spiros. *The Complete Word Study Dictionary of the New Testament.* Chattanooga: AMG Publishers 1992

Zuck, Roy B. - Ed. *A Biblical Theology of the New Testament.* Chicago: Moody 1994

Zuck, Roy B. - Ed. *A Biblical Theology of the Old Testament.* Chicago: Moody 1991

Zuck, Roy B. *The Bible Knowledge Commentary 2 Vol. Set.* Colorado Springs: Victor 1983

Also Available:

Simple Theology:
Theology for the Rest of Us
Dr. Clay A. Kahler

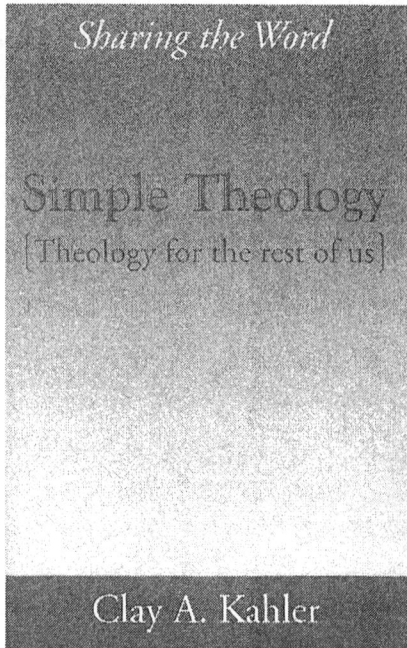

This survey of theology is suited for every believer, regardless of previous knowledge or spiritual maturity. Dr. Kahler presents theological truths in a way that is easy to understand and will spur the reader on to further study.

ISBN: 1579108873

Available from Christian bookstores and online book sellers nationwide.

Against Protestant Popes:
An Exegetical Study of 1 Peter 5:1-4 (Paperback)
Dr. Clay A. Kahler

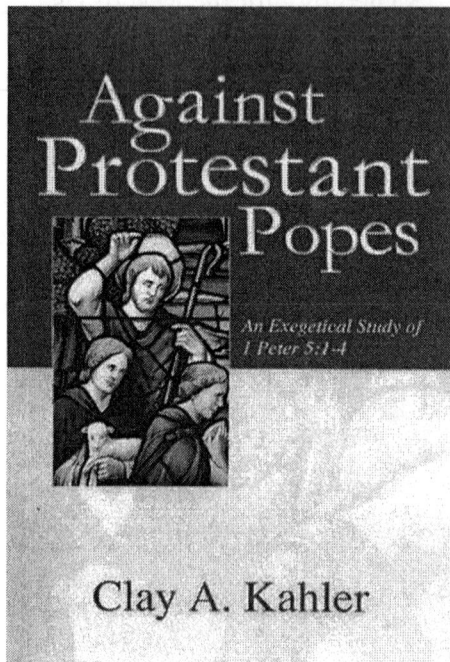

A BIBLICAL LOOK at God's awesome call to be a shepherd
to His flock. This exegetical look at Peter's admonition to
"fellow Shepherds" will cause those in ministry to look very
hard at their own model of ministry. Packed full of Biblical
insights, this is a must read for all of those in or
considering the ministry.

ISBN: 1597521493

Available from Christian bookstores and online book sellers nationwide.

The Irreducible Minimum:
An Examination of Basic Christian Doctrine
Dr. David C. Myers

the irreducible minimum
An examination of basic Christian doctrine

David C. Myers

Dr. Myers' book, "The Irreducible Minimum" is a must read
book for anyone interested in a survey of classic Christian
doctrine. This book is great for individual study as well as
Bible study or Sunday School groups.
Get this book and enter into the world of Biblical doctrine with
this great seminary professor and pastor as your guide.

ISBN: 1579102794

Available from Christian bookstores and online book sellers nationwide.

www.ingramcontent.com/pod-product-compliance
Lightning Source LLC
Chambersburg PA
CBHW071109090426
42737CB00013B/2542